In the Tub

by Andrew Kasparyan
illustrated by John Hinderliter

C0-BKZ-785

Harcourt
SCHOOL PUBLISHERS

Requests for permission to make copies of any part of the work should be addressed to School Permissions and Copyrights, Harcourt, Inc., 6277 Sea Harbor Drive, Orlando, Florida 32887–6777. Fax: 407-345-2418.

HARCOURT and the Harcourt Logo are trademarks of Harcourt, Inc., registered in the United States of America and/or other jurisdictions.

Printed in Mexico

ISBN 10: 0-15-358414-9
ISBN 13: 978-0-15-358414-5

Ordering Options
ISBN 10: 0-15-358356-8 (Grade K On-Level Collection)
ISBN 13: 978-0-15-358356-8 (Grade K On-Level Collection)
ISBN 10: 0-15-360666-5 (package of 5)
ISBN 13: 978-0-15-360666-3 (package of 5)

2 3 4 5 6 7 8 9 10 050 15 14 13 12 11 10 09 08 07

Get in the tub, Cub.
We can rub off the mud.

I will get a mat.
I will get a rag.

Get in the tub, Cub.
You have to go in there.

I will get my sub and Rex.
I will get my cup.

Get in the tub, Cub.
It is not hot.

Look at that in the tub!
I will not get in!

I see what is in the tub.
It is Pup!